A WORKBOOK FOR ADULTS

Designed to accompany
Rebel Badge Book Volume One

by Charly Lester

April 2022

Over the last six months the Rebel Badge Club has grown
rapidly in numbers, and I've been watching all the ways you've
charted your progress. It's been an absolute pleasure to see
everyone get so excited and passionate about an idea I had
mowing my lawn one day! Thank you all for your enthusiasm,
and for 'spreading the Rebel love'.

A number of people have been adding their stickers to dotted
journals, and asked if I could create a special workbook to
accompany the first volume of Rebel Badge Book, so here it is!
We've created a sheet of special stickers to accompany this
book, and you can find them, together with all the latest Rebel
badges and goodies, at www.rebelbadgestore.com

Thanks and enjoy!
Charly

First published 2022
Edition Two - 2023

Rebel Badge Book and Rebel Badge Club are trademarks of Charly Lester Ltd.
www.rebelbadgebook.com

ARTIST

MAKE SOMETHING BEAUTIFUL

Use these pages for your art creations, scrapbook or to plan.

DATE COMPLETED:

CRAFT PART ONE

START YOU CREATIVE JOURNEY

Use these pages for badge planning, or add photos of your craft projects.

DATE COMPLETED:

CRITIC
SPEAK YOUR MIND

Use these pages to write your 5 reviews:

CRITIC

CRITIC

DATE COMPLETED:

DANCER
FEEL THE BEAT

Use these pages for Clauses 2 and 3.

DATE COMPLETED:

DESIGNER

SEW UP A STORM

Use the pages for clauses 4, 5 and 6.

DATE COMPLETED:

FLORIST
BRIGHTEN UP A ROOM

REBEL

DATE COMPLETED:

MUSICIAN

MAKE SOME MUSIC

DATE COMPLETED:

PHOTOGRAPHER
CAPTURE THE BEAUTY

PHOTOGRAPHER

DATE COMPLETED:

WRITER
PUT PEN TO PAPER

Plan your writing project on these pages

WRITER

DATE COMPLETED:

ACTIVIST

STAND UP FOR WHAT YOU BELIEVE IN

DATE COMPLETED:

ANIMAL LOVER
ALL CREATURES GREAT & SMALL

DATE COMPLETED:

COMMUNITY SERVICE
TIME TO HELP OUT

DATE COMPLETED:

CONSCIOUS CONSUMER

THINK BEFORE YOU BUY

DATE COMPLETED:

EMERGENCY HELPER

BE PREPARED

DATE COMPLETED:

ENTREPRENEUR
START-UP TIME

DATE COMPLETED:

ENVIRONMENTALIST

LET'S PRESERVE OUR WORLD

REBEL

DATE COMPLETED:

FUNDRAISER

SUPPORT GOOD CAUSES

DATE COMPLETED:

DATE COMPLETED:

WORLD TRAVELLER

EXPLORE THE WORLD

DATE COMPLETED:

ADULTING

ACCEPT SOME RESPONSIBILITIES

Add your 6 chosen chores below and tick off when complete. ✓

DATE COMPLETED:

BAKER

NO SOGGY BOTTOMS HERE!

Tick off your progress in the relevant section

3 TYPES OF BREAD	3 TYPES OF CAKE	3 TYPES OF BISCUIT

CLASSIC PUDDING	SAVOURY PIE	ECLAIRS

SWEET TART	BATCH BAKE	MILLE-FEUILLE

DATE COMPLETED:

CHEF
COOK UP A STORM

Record the dates you complete each task:

01

02

03

04

05

06

07

08

09

DATE COMPLETED:

DIY

ROLL UP THOSE SLEEVES

Check off the 8 tasks as you complete them

01

02

03

04

05

06

07

08

DATE COMPLETED:

EVENT PLANNER
YOU'RE IN CHARGE

PRE-EVENT

LAST MINUTE

ON THE DAY

POST EVENT

EVENT PLANNER

Event Checklist

REBEL

PRE-EVENT

○
○
○
○
○

LAST MINUTE

○
○
○
○
○

ON THE DAY

○
○
○
○

POST EVENT

○
○
○
○

EVENT PLANNER

Event Checklist

REBEL

PRE-EVENT

LAST MINUTE

ON THE DAY

POST EVENT

DATE COMPLETED:

GARDENER
GET GREEN FINGERS

Tick off and date each clause when you complete it

01

02

03

04

05

06

07

08

DATE COMPLETED:

INDOOR GARDENER

LET'S TALK TO SOME PLANTS

DATE COMPLETED:

INTERIOR DESIGNER

DECORATE YOUR SPACE

DATE COMPLETED:

INVESTOR

LEARN TO MAKE YOUR MONEY COUNT

DATE COMPLETED:

MECHANIC

GET YOUR MOTOR RUNNING

DATE COMPLETED:

MONEY SAVER

EVERY PENNY COUNTS

DATE COMPLETED:

MY BRAND

TIME FOR SOME PERSONAL BRANDING

 **MY BRAND**

As part of the My Brand badge, evaluate the following qualities. Are there any you'd like to improve on?

Self Belief

1	2	3	4	5	6	7	8	9	10

Positive Mental Attitude

1	2	3	4	5	6	7	8	9	10

Flexibility

1	2	3	4	5	6	7	8	9	10

Decision Making

1	2	3	4	5	6	7	8	9	10

Determination

1	2	3	4	5	6	7	8	9	10

Desire to Learn and Grow

1	2	3	4	5	6	7	8	9	10

MY BRAND

MY BRAND

Now choose your own qualities and rate them.
Again, are there any you'd like to focus on improving?

....

| 1 | 2 | 3 | 4 | 5 | 6 | 7 | 8 | 9 | 10 |

....

| 1 | 2 | 3 | 4 | 5 | 6 | 7 | 8 | 9 | 10 |

....

| 1 | 2 | 3 | 4 | 5 | 6 | 7 | 8 | 9 | 10 |

....

| 1 | 2 | 3 | 4 | 5 | 6 | 7 | 8 | 9 | 10 |

....

| 1 | 2 | 3 | 4 | 5 | 6 | 7 | 8 | 9 | 10 |

....

| 1 | 2 | 3 | 4 | 5 | 6 | 7 | 8 | 9 | 10 |

DATE COMPLETED:

REBEL

MY GOALS

WHERE DO YOU WANT TO BE?

Start by identifying at least one goal for the next 6-12 months for each of the areas below.

Over the next 3 months use the worksheets to break down your goals into actionable tasks and make positive changes to your life.

HEALTH	CAREER	WEALTH

TRAVEL	FAMILY	LIFESTYLE

CREATIVITY	KNOWLEDGE	RELATIONSHIPS

GOAL TRACKER

Monthly Goals :

Weekly Goals :

	1
	2
	3
	4

GOAL TRACKER

Monthly Goals :

Weekly Goals :

	1
	2
	3
	4

GOAL TRACKER

Monthly Goals :

Weekly Goals :

1

2

3

4

DATE COMPLETED:

MY ROOTS

EXPLORE YOUR FAMILY TREE

DATE COMPLETED:

MY STYLE

REVIEW YOUR WARDROBE

DATE COMPLETED:

MY TALENTS

BE YOUR OWN BIGGEST FAN

DATE COMPLETED:

APOTHECARY

MIX UP A STORM

DATE COMPLETED:

DIARIST

HOW DO YOU FEEL?

DATE COMPLETED:

FITNESS

GET ACTIVE!

DATE COMPLETED:

GOOD HABITS

GET IN THE SWING OF THINGS

DATE COMPLETED:

Fitness Tracker
Month 1

Month: _____   Target Number of Days : _____

Use the tracker below to record every day of exercise you complete this month. You may wish to count the days as you go along, use crosses when you exercise, or add dates to the days.

MONTHLY GOALS

MON	TUE	WED	THU	FRI	SAT	SUN

Fitness Tracker
Month 2

Month:

Target Number of Days :

Use the tracker below to record every day of exercise you complete this month. You may wish to count the days as you go along, use crosses when you exercise, or add dates to the days.

MONTHLY GOALS

MON	TUE	WED	THU	FRI	SAT	SUN

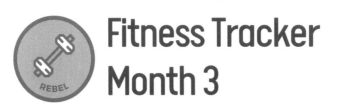

Fitness Tracker
Month 3

Month: _____   Target Number of Days : _____

Use the tracker below to record every day of exercise you complete this month. You may wish to count the days as you go along, use crosses when you exercise, or add dates to the days.

MONTHLY GOALS

MON	TUE	WED	THU	FRI	SAT	SUN

Monthly Log

LIFE ADMIN HABIT:

HEALTH AND FITNESS HABIT:

HOUSEHOLD HABIT:

SELF CARE HABIT:

TRACKER

MON	TUE	WED	THU	FRI	SAT	SUN

Monthly Log

LIFE ADMIN HABIT:

HEALTH AND FITNESS HABIT:

HOUSEHOLD HABIT:

SELF CARE HABIT:

TRACKER

MON	TUE	WED	THU	FRI	SAT	SUN

Monthly Log

LIFE ADMIN HABIT:

HEALTH AND FITNESS HABIT:

HOUSEHOLD HABIT:

SELF CARE HABIT:

TRACKER

MON	TUE	WED	THU	FRI	SAT	SUN

MINDFULNESS

BE PRESENT IN THE MOMENT

DATE COMPLETED:

READER

PAGE BY PAGE

DATE COMPLETED:

RUNNER
ONE STEP AT A TIME

DATE COMPLETED:

SELF CARE

BE YOUR OWN BEST FRIEND

DATE COMPLETED:

ADVENTURER

MAKE THE MOST OF THE OUTDOORS

DATE COMPLETED:

CAMPER

NIGHTS UNDER CANVAS

DATE COMPLETED:

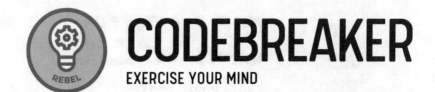

CODEBREAKER

EXERCISE YOUR MIND

DATE COMPLETED:

EXPLORER
NAVIGATE YOU OWN WAY

DATE COMPLETED:

OUTDOOR COOK

STRIKE UP THE FIRE

DATE COMPLETED:

STARGAZER

LOOK TO THE SKY

This badge is dedicated to Bob Lester.

STARGAZER:

This badge is dedicated to Bob Lester.

DATE COMPLETED:

SURVIVOR

FEND FOR YOURSELF

DATE COMPLETED:

WATER SPORTS

GET IN THE SPLASH ZONE

DATE COMPLETED:

WILD SWIMMER

TIME TO GET WET!

DATE COMPLETED:

CHALLENGES

CHALLENGES

CHALLENGES

CHALLENGES

BADGE TRACKER

CROSS OFF EACH BADGE AS YOU EARN IT OR ADD STICKERS

BADGE TRACKER

CROSS OFF EACH BADGE AS YOU EARN IT OR ADD STICKERS

Made in United States
Troutdale, OR
10/11/2023